GREAT
BATHROOMS

Great Bathrooms

Produced by Jeffrey Weiss
Text by Susan Rayfield
Design by R.J. Luzzi
Photography by Janis Tracy Andrus, Jon Elliot, David Fraser, Nick Gunderson, Michael Kanouff, David Leach, Toby Richards
St. Martin's Press
New York

Copyright © 1981 by Jeffrey Weiss Group, Inc.
For information, write: St. Martin's Press,
175 Fifth Avenue, New York, N.Y. 10010
Printed in Hong Kong by the South China Printing Co.

Design by R.J. Luzzi
10 9 8 7 6 5 4 3 2 1
First Edition

Library of Congress Cataloging in Publication Data

Friedman-Weiss, Jeffrey.
   Great bathrooms.

   1. Bathrooms. 2. Interior decoration.
I. Title.
NK2117.B33F74   747.7'8   80-29135
ISBN 0-312-34486-4

GREAT BATHROOMS

Whether you want to give your old bathroom a quick facelift, plan major improvements, or design a new one from scratch, here are many inexpensive, exciting ideas that will help you turn it into a sleek, dramatic showcase.

In one weekend, for very little money, you can give your bathroom—even in a cramped, dimly-lit efficiency apartment—a bright new look. If you own your home and have more money to invest, you will discover how to expand the space and what to look for in new fixtures. And if you are about to construct a new room, we will show you how to build the bathroom of tomorrow—today.

Once the dullest and most uncomfortable room in the house, the bathroom has finally come into its own. The cold floor has been covered with plush carpeting, dingy walls transformed with bright wallpapers and mirrors, track lighting has replaced weak bulbs, and the old white fixtures have given way to streamlined, colorful matching units. Add a few plants, paintings, magazines, fresh flowers and a sound system, and you have the elements of a luxurious retreat—a place to unwind, relax and escape from the day's tensions. And if you think that creating a room like those shown in these pages must be time-consuming and prohibitively expensive—not so! Ready-to-assemble materials and installation kits make much of the updating and remodeling easy to do yourself, at a fraction of the cost a contractor would charge.

Here are some points to consider before you begin:

Function: How many people will be using the room, including children and the elderly? A one-bath home with a multibath-needs family might call for installing a double sink and building a privacy wall between tub and toilet so that more than one person can use the facilities at the same time.

Space: If you are planning to increase the available space and rip out fixtures, make a sketch of the room with the new equipment in place. Measure wall length, width of windows and doors, size and shape of the fixtures, position of electrical outlets, radiators, etc., and transfer to graph paper, on a scale of ½-inch-to-1-foot. Try to arrange all of the fixtures along one wall, with the sink closest to the door. The typical room plans in this book will give you some ideas.

Appearance: Decide on the style of the room—modern, country, nostalgic, Oriental—and then choose the colors that you want to dominate and those needed for decorative accents. Get color swatches of different materials and see how they work together.

Cost: Friends or a local architect can advise you regarding reliable contractors. Obtain several estimates and compare the prices of different manufacturers at a number of supply stores. Consider total costs—fixtures, installation, maintenance and operation.

Safety: A bathroom's wet, slippery surfaces can be hazardous. Install grab bars, 40″ high at the tub, shoulder height in the shower. Make sure tub and shower have non-skid bottoms and keep electrical outlets at least three feet away from water-supply fixtures.

Codes: A building permit is required for a new bathroom and new plumbing, and the work must conform to local building codes. Ask your building inspector about it *before* you start.

Walls and Ceilings

Bathroom walls can be painted, papered, paneled, tiled or covered with fabric, glass or mirrors. What you decide to do depends on the condition of the walls, the proportions of the room and your own personal taste.

If the walls are in bad shape and you are doing extensive remodeling, you will probably want to tear them down. However, if the walls are in good condition you may be able to cover them with a new finish after they have appear lower. Then again, you may decide to have fun with what you can't hide and accent the pipes in bright, contrasting colors for an interesting hi-tech effect. Plaids or stripes will help unite a room with awkward angles and will provide a good background for displaying solid-color objects, such as a plate collection.

Paint

An oil-based (or "alkyd") paint adheres better to moist walls and ceilings than latex (or "water-based") paint. For a long-lasting job, buy a high-quality product and use two full coats. Walls painted with a glossy finish are easier to clean than those with a flat finish. Waterproof epoxy paint will cover discolored tiles, tubs and the worn chrome of faucets with a hard coat that will last for years.

Fabric

Apply fabric to walls or cabinets with wallpaper paste and, since it absorbs moisture, seal it with a coat of shellac for waterproofing. Shirred fabric, gathered and hung on curtain rods mounted at the floor and ceiling, can be used to hide walls in very poor condition.

Wallpaper

Covering the walls with paper will give your bathroom a bright new look overnight. Also try papering the sides of the tub and trim around the mirror or medicine cabinet. You can tie the decorative scheme of the room together by using a reverse pattern for the window shade and sink skirt, and coordinated fabrics are available for shower or window curtains.

Multiply the width of each wall by its height in feet (subtracting the area taken up by the window and door) to determine the total square feet to be covered. You may have to steam off worn and peeling paper and remove the old paste. Then remove any molding and paint the trim. Coat the walls with sizing or a resin sealer to prevent the new paste from soaking into the wall. If the under surface is rough and uneven, apply lining paper first to smooth out the bumps. When you hang the wallpaper, make certain the pattern is right side up; use a carpenter's level or plumb bob to be sure the panels are vertically straight; and match the repeat exactly—the smallest errors show up on papered walls.

Wood

Paneling is rich-looking and easy to care for and has become increasingly popular in bathrooms. Redwood, which resists moisture, is an excellent foil for shiny brass fittings. Rough-textured cedar or pine siding gives a rustic, out-of-doors feeling. Be sure to protect any wood surface with several coats of polyurethane. If the bathroom has old and drab wainscoting, however, you may have to cover dark wood with acrylic paint; light wood panels can be dyed with an aniline stain that alters the color but retains the grain of the wood.

been patched up, cleaned, thoroughly dried and sealed with a primer. By mixing color and texture, you can create any look you want. A rainbow of solid colors is available as well as prints, paisleys, stripes, geometrics, flower and free-form patterns. You may want to combine tiles and fabric, wood and wallpaper or paint and mirrors. To expand a small room visually or give the ceiling more height, choose light colors or reflective paper. Dark hues will camouflage poor walls, a tangle of unsightly pipes or an old radiator, and will make the ceiling

Tiles

Use a flat pry bar to remove old tiles, then repair and smooth the bare wallboards with joint compound, apply adhesive and set in the new tiles. Many are now pre-grouted so that sections of up to 36 tiles can be installed at one time. Select one of the many bright colors available, or a checkerboard pattern that will contrast with the white grouting. Handpainted Mexican, Portuguese or French-glazed tiles provide a decorative accent and nowadays you can even have fabric laminated and used as tiles. For a more unusual wallcovering, you might consider dark glass panels, chrome, mirrors, strips of beaten glass, cork or slate.

Floors

The floor brings the whole design of the bathroom together. If the existing surface is too poor to salvage, rip it up, nail down plywood strips and cover them with the new flooring. Tiles provide the ideal waterproof surface and are still the most popular floor covering for bathrooms. They should be slightly rough-surfaced to prevent slipping. If porcelain tile seems too cold and clinical, wall-to-wall carpeting is a popular solution; it warms up the room both literally and visually. Wood floors provide a warm, natural-looking surface. They can also be painted or stained, and should be waterproofed with polish or polyurethane. A clear seal will bring out the grain; white seal will produce a bleached look. Other floor coverings include brick (especially attractive with rough-hewn cedar walls), textured rubber matting or cork. Avoid pure white or very dark floors as they tend to show dirt.

Windows

If you are fortunate enough to have a bathroom with a view, it can be treated as the focal point. A plant-filled bay window lends a light and airy look. You can buy pre-assembled greenhouse windows, which usually come divided into small panes, or have your own custom-built, complete with Lucite or glass shelves. Frame a narrow window with books and art objects, then add a tall vase with a single flower to emphasize its shape.

Sometimes, however, a window can be an eyesore that imperils privacy. If this is the case, you can frost the lower panes, insert a piece of stained glass or replace the window with tinted or translucent glass to filter the light. If the view needs to be blocked altogether, attractive horizontal or vertical matchstick blinds, patterned shades, or painted shutters can transform the bleakest window into a pleasing part of the room.

Lighting

A bathroom should have at least two sources of artificial light—a bright spot over the lavatory for grooming, and a more diffuse type of lighting for the rest of the room. Strips of tiny track lighting or theatrical bulbs are effective around the mirror and add a modern touch. Tracks are an excellent way of getting a lot of light from one outlet without extra, expensive electrical work. You can install a dimmer switch to alter their intensity and change the mood. Frosted globes on either side of the lavatory give a soft, flattering glow. Recess spotlights in the ceiling or conceal them behind a valance running along the edge of the room, substituting grow lamps for regular bulbs wherever there are areas of greenery. If you are remodeling a room, plan for a continuous outlet strip above the sink's splashback to accommodate the small appliances that you use in the bathroom.

Translucent panels in the ceiling or over the tub provide more diffuse lighting. Hide fluorescent tubes beneath a dropped ceiling above the tub area, masking them with a panel of plexiglass. The tubes give three times as much light as ordinary bulbs and last much longer, so they are more economical to use where high levels of light are required for longer periods of time. Install a combination light/heat/air vent over the shower or tub to prevent shadow and fogging.

Storage

In most bathrooms, storage space is either non-existent or poorly planned. How many times have you groped for a towel, eyes stinging with shampoo, or stepped into the shower to discover that the soap was ten chilly feet away? A shelf along the side of the tub or recessed in the shower stall will keep bath supplies within easy reach.

Bathrooms are usually so small that every nook and corner must be considered as storage space. Cabinets and shelves can be placed over the toilet, shower and tub, under the sink and along both sides of the mirror. The most widely used and best-known way to add storage space is a vanity-lavatory combination, in which the sink basin is dropped into a countertop with built-in cabinets below. To gain more space, and avoid the pipes, extend the vanity beyond the basin as far as possible. Cover open shelves with a sink skirt.

A medicine cabinet over the lavatory will add more storage space and should be as wide as the vanity below. You can also build small cubicles around the cabinet or central mirror to store tall bottles, a portable hairdryer, small radio and other items. If you have the space, floor-to-ceiling open shelves on brackets are easy to install. Another possibility for adding storage space is to break through the wall to an existing closet. A privacy wall, usually built to separate the tub area from the toilet, is a good storage unit. Its hollow interior serves as a cabinet, the sides support towel racks and rings, and the two-level top can be used to display plants.

If you are squeezed for space, vertical hotel towel racks are practical, as are retractable racks that pull out for use as drying rods. Heated racks are useful when there isn't much room for stretching out wet towels. Wooden double-loop ship rails, available at marine supply stores, make unusual towel racks and you can even hang towels from a garden trellis mounted flush to the wall. Consider portable storage units for laundry, such as a wicker hamper on wheels or an industrial steel trash can, with a swinging top.

Fixtures

You don't have to remove the existing fixtures to remodel your outmoded bathroom. A ball and claw tub, pull-chain toilet and pedestal sink can add considerable charm, and a few coats of bright epoxy paint will give this old equipment a new lease on life. In fact remodeling backwards—to make a bathroom look old rather than modern —is in style now, and some of the leading plumbingware manufacturers are featuring newly built models of turn-of-the-century fixtures.

If your bathroom was built too late to qualify for quaintness, however, you will find many new bathroom components to choose from, in colors ranging from pastels to bright tones and unusual decorator shades. Be sure to select a color that you won't tire of easily; once installed, the bathroom fixtures will be there for a long time.

Bathtub

Not so long ago, if you wanted a new tub, you would buy a traditional white fixture, 5 feet long, 30 inches wide and 14 inches deep. Today, bathtubs can be oval, round, triangular, square or free-form. You can select one that is extra long, for stretching out in luxurious comfort, extra wide to accommodate broad shoulders, or extra deep, for those who like to immerse themselves up to the chin for a good soak. The tub can be a space-saving corner unit, installed in the conventional recess, built as a peninsula jutting out from the wall or set up as an island in the center of the room. All models, especially the free-standing ones, can be enclosed in wood paneling or tiles, with a wide surround for storing bath equipment or toys.

Traditional tubs are enameled steel or enameled cast iron, but tubs are now also made of rigid fiberglass which can be molded with a headrest, sloping back support and textured, non-skid bottom. The new one-piece fiberglass units are easy for do-it-yourselfers to install. They are not as heavy as the steel and cast-iron kinds, and, although they are priced slightly higher, the price is offset by lower installation costs. Some are designed for new construction rather than remodeling, since they are too large to fit through the average 32-inch doorway unless the door and jamb are removed. But several models now come in four-piece knockdown units— tub and three wall sections—for assembly in place. Usually the pipes from the old tub can be reconnected, if they are in good condition and properly positioned.

Many bathtubs come with luxury attachments, such as water and air jets for whirlpool action, and tub-sauna combinations are also available. Hot tubs heat aerated water up to 110° F and have become so popular that bathing has become a social event, with indoor-outdoor spas built large enough to accommodate the whole family. For the ultimate in luxury, you can own the Habitat by Kohler, an enclosed environment about 7 feet long, 5 feet high and 4 feet deep. Open the sliding glass door, lie down on the cedar planks and experience 20 minutes of sun, rain and steam in automatic sequence, with warm air added to simulate rolling mist or a desert breeze. A built-in sound system completes the sybaritic experience. Whether you add jazzy color to an old tub and bathe by candlelight, immerse yourself in swirling bubbles or join a tub party, one thing's for sure—the old Saturday night bath will never be the same again.

Showers

Conventional shower units are 32- or 36-inches square, and come with glass doors or rods for curtains. Some showers that connect rooms can be open on two sides, for walk-through convenience. Today's trend favors a more open look, and when the stall is high enough to prevent splashing, you can add depth to the room by eliminating the shower curtain. If the shower is in a corner, surrounded by tiled walls and floor, you don't even need a stall.

Many different shower attachments are now available. Hand-held, pulsating massagers have adjustable sprays, from fine to coarse, with sheeting action for washing hair. One unit spurts tingling jets of hot or cold water from all sides, another will convert the shower into a steam cabinet.

Sink

In addition to enameled steel and the more expensive but chip-resistant enameled cast iron, sinks are also made of vitreous china, which is top-of-the-line because of its gleaming finish and sleek styling. They come as standing pedestals, wall-hung models or basins with an integral surround and splashback. One modular unit has a built-in light, mirror and shelf. Installing a stainless steel kitchen sink in a bathroom will give it a modern, industrial look; hand-carved marble or ceramic sinks with floral designs are high-priced luxury items.

The sink should be deep enough for washing hair and wide enough to prevent splattering. For maximum comfort, set it between 34 and 36 inches high, which is higher than the conventional sink. Double sinks are a practical investment when several people share one bath.

Toilet

The standard toilet size is 20- to 22-inches wide at the tank, extending 27 inches from the wall, although many different sizes and shapes are now available. Be sure to check the quality of the flush mechanism inside the tank and since toilet noise is caused by water rushing through narrow passages, select one with a wide drain basin. The quietest and most efficient toilet is the siphon jet, with tank water discharged through jets around the rim of the bowl. Toilets now come with no-overflow and self-ventilating features. Water-saver models use one-third less water per flush; wall-hung units are easier to clean around. For the European touch, add a bidet—a natural companion fixture to any toilet.

The style of your bathroom can be keynoted by the faucets, handles and trim that you select. Since they are subject to constant use, they should be sturdy and functional. A contemporary fitting with a single, round control will look streamlined but may be difficult for children to manipulate. Fittings are measured from center to center of each valve and come in two widths, 4-inch and 8-inch, regardless of whether the handles and faucets are one unit (centerset) or in three pieces (widespread set). The controls are available in compact single, standard double or combination models. Most fittings are made of brass plated with chrome, brass, gold or pewter. The handles can be metal, enamel, acrylic, wood or a decorative stone, such as onyx.

Accessories

Your bathroom is an intimate retreat that should be full of surprises and small luxuries. Color accents are important and can be provided by an imaginative display of towels—piled flat on acrylic shelves, rolled up in straw or wire baskets or stuffed into long drainage tiles to form a brilliant honeycomb.

Greenery such as ferns, philodendron, staghorn and spider plants, thrive in the moist, heated environment and add a softening touch. Hang them from the ceiling, mass them at the window, place a tall plant in a corner or even a vase of fresh flowers on the vanity.

Photographs, paintings, collages and wallhangings all add interest to the room and help to create atmosphere. For an unusual touch, display memorabilia, such as items from a Victorian lady's wardrobe or a collection of old bottles, plates, or antique dolls. Bring in magazines and some of your favorite books. If space is available, reserve a corner for a mat, some exercise equipment and a sunlamp.

Use your own personal style and inventiveness to make the most of the room in which you spend up to ten percent of your time. Today's wide range of colors, materials and finishes makes it possible to combine convenience and economy with exciting design so the bathroom can be anything you want it to be, from country casual to sleek and sophisticated. It is no longer just a bathroom, but a luxurious room with a bath.

WHERE TO GET MORE INFORMATION

American Olean Tile, Lansdale, Pa. 19446
American Standard, Box 2003, New Brunswick, NJ 08903
Borg-Warner Corp., Plumbing Products Division, 20 East 5th, Mansfield, Ohio 44910
Country Floors
Crane Co., 300 Park Ave., New York, NY 10022
Eljer Plumbingware, 3 Gateway Center, Pittsburgh, Pa. 15222
Hastings, 964 Third Ave., New York, NY 10022
Hastings Tile, 410 Lakeville Road, Lake Success, NY 11040
Jacuzzi, Drawer J, Walnut Creek, Ca. 94596
Kohler Co., Kohler, Wisconsin 53044
Owens-Corning Fiberlgas, Fiberglass Tower, Toledo, Ohio 43659
Powers-Fiat, 3400 Oakton St., Skokie, Ill. 60076
Sherle Wagner, 60 E. 57th St., New York, NY 10022
Universal-Rundle, New Castle, Pa. 16103

14

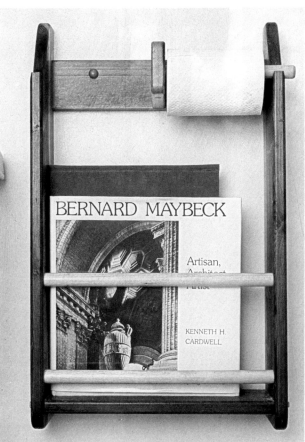

26

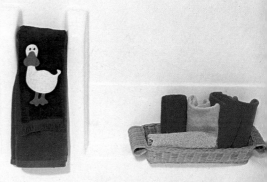

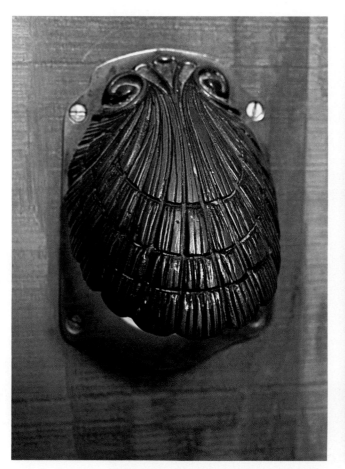

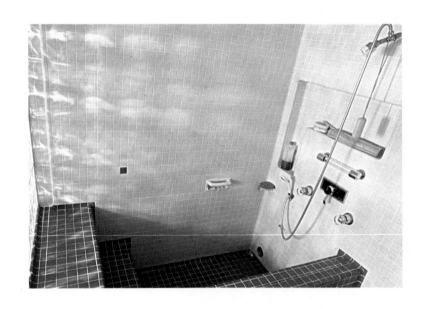

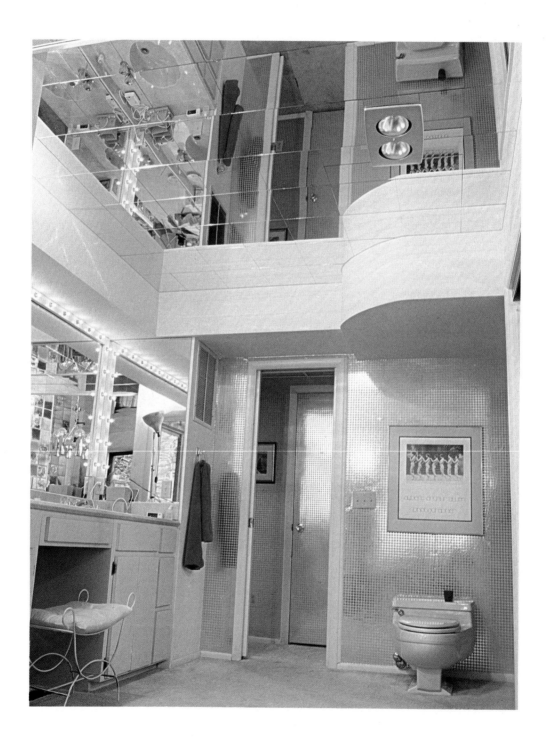

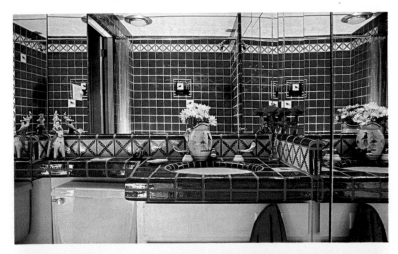

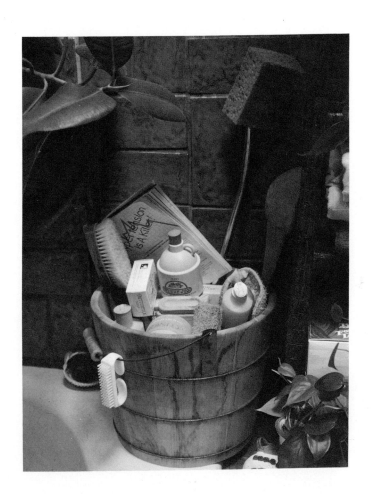

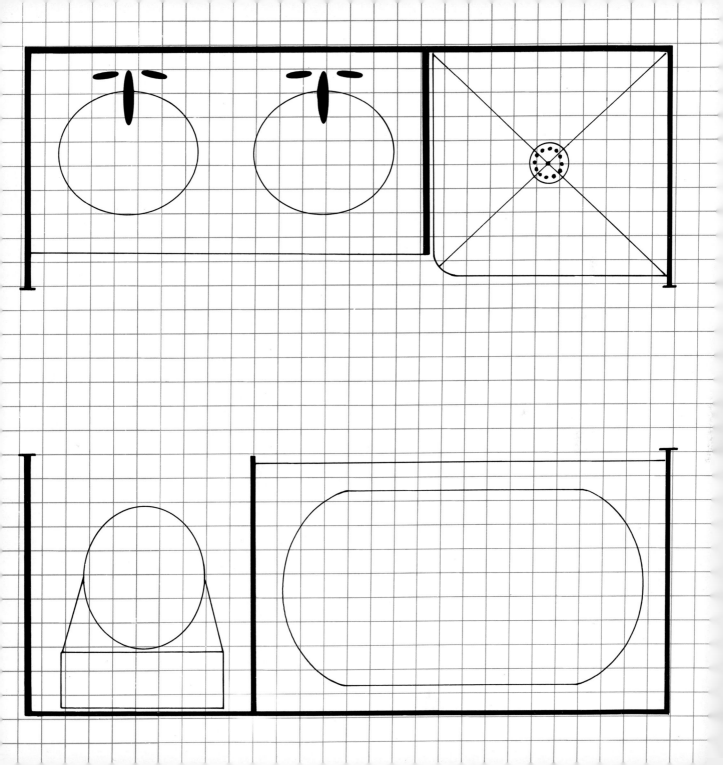

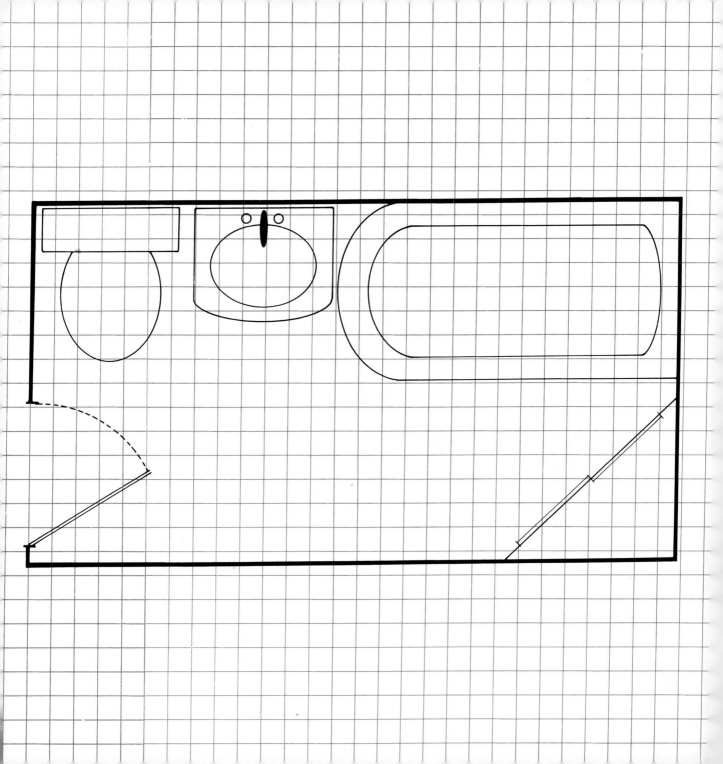

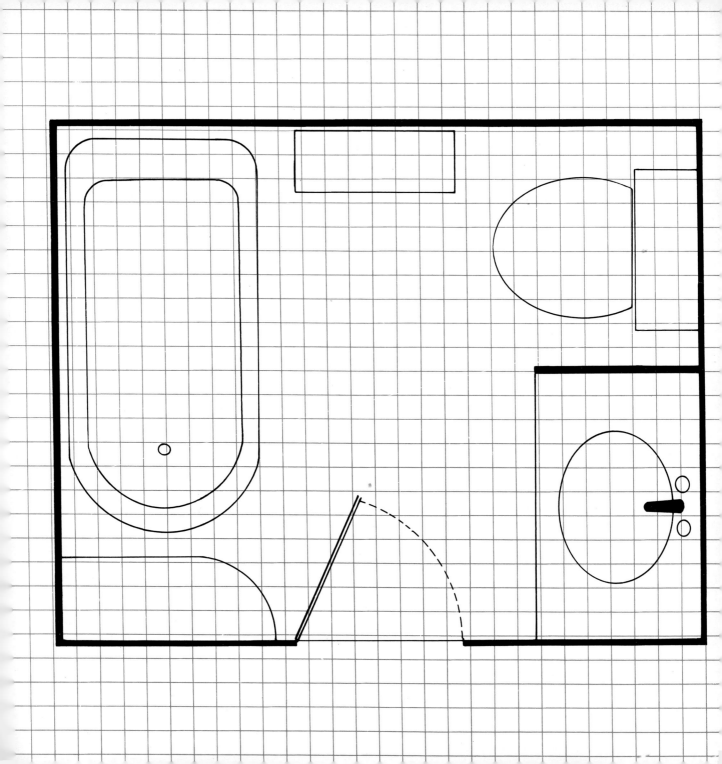

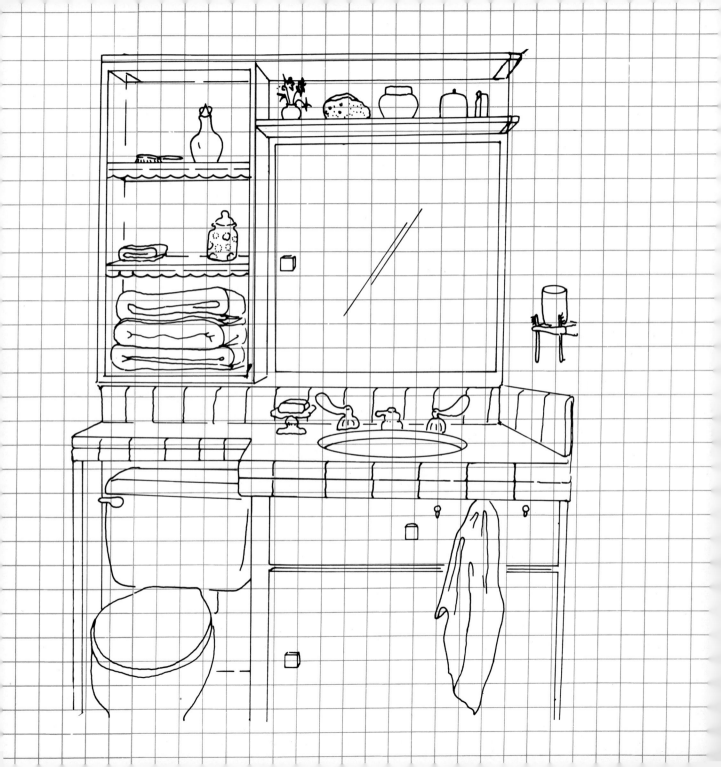

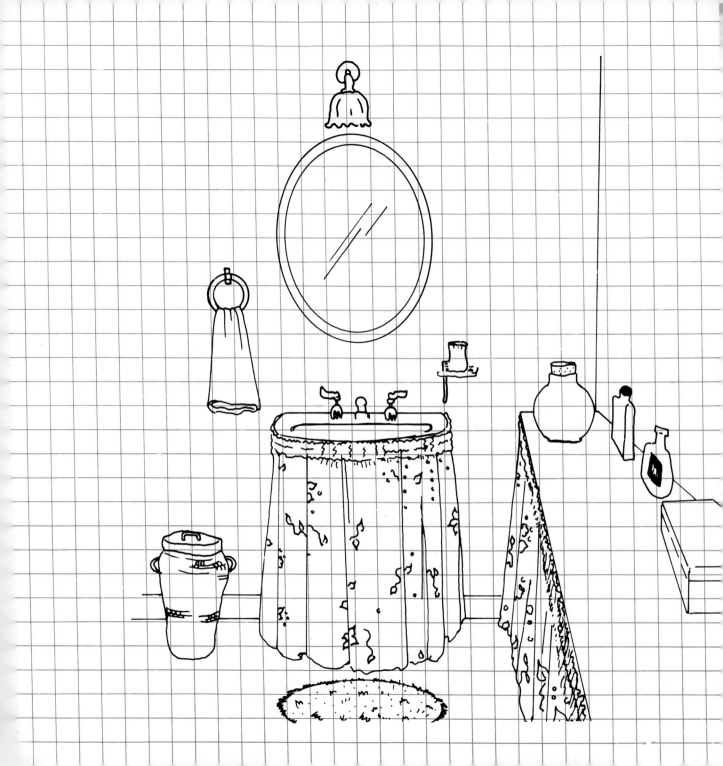

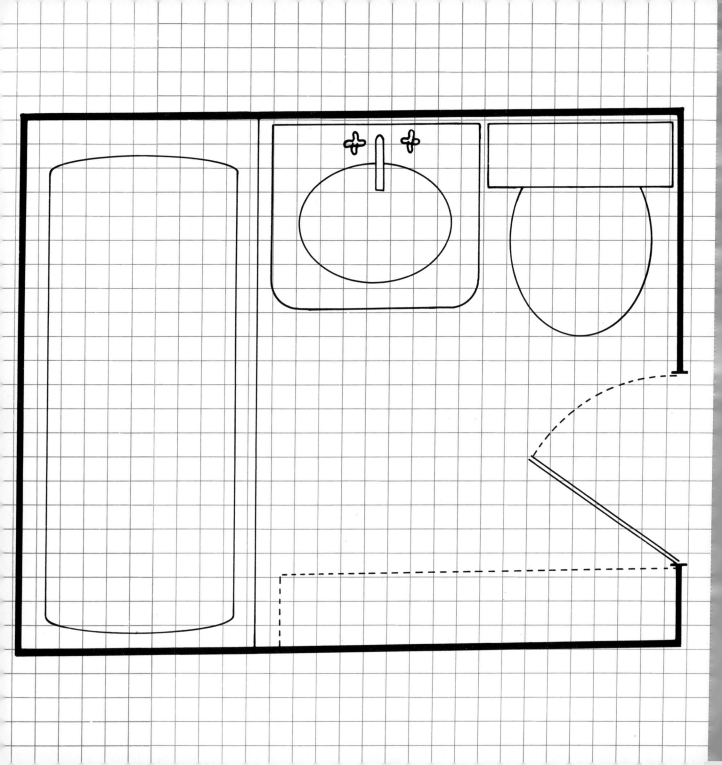

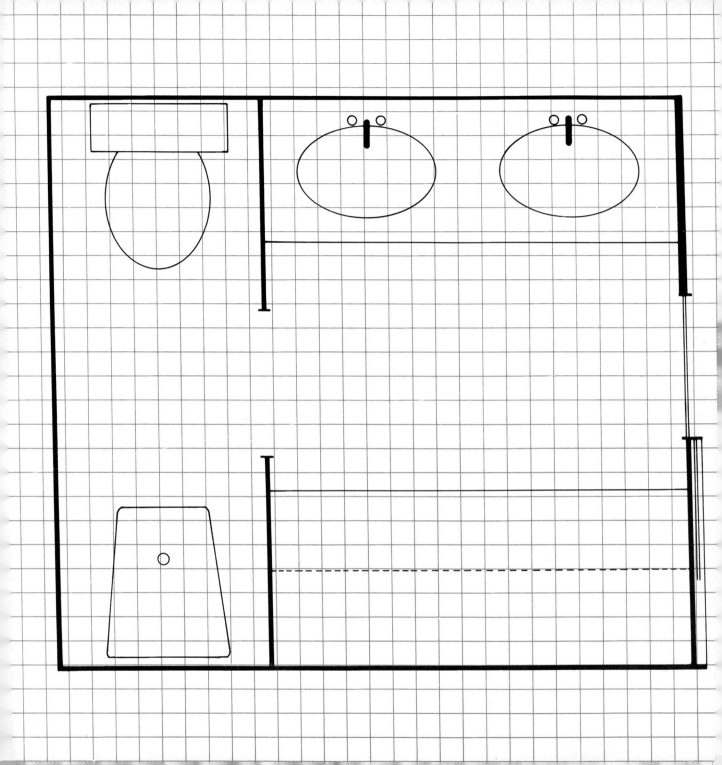

CREDITS

Designed by Calvin Ashford
of Gilmore-Ashford Power
Design, Inc.   16

Judith Carrington   72–73

Georgio DeLuca   18–19

Clay Eaton   46–47

Caleb and Susan Foote   24–27

Alvin Kahn   51

Mary Sims   38–41

Special thanks to Judith Barrett, Judith Carrington, Karen Graul

Illustrations by Deborah Bracken

We would like to express our deep appreciation to those owners and designers that allowed us to photograph their homes and wished to remain anonymous.